BHARATNATYAM ADAVU GROUP 1

TATTADAVU

SWARNIKA

Contents

CHAPTER ONE

TATTADAVU

Tattadavus are the basic footsteps that involve striking of the feet in Aramandi posture. This is the first adavu that dancers learn. Dancers get acquainted with hand-leg coordination, hand gestures along with eyes, head, neck and torso movements. The footwork uses complete 'thaap',i.e. the foot striking the floor completely.

Tattadavu in general has eight steps that is perfomed in three speeds. Dancers performing at advanced level perform this adavu in Anudhurita laya (fourth speed) also. Different banis tend to have slight moderations in either bol or footwork pattern, sometimes both.

There have been two major variations in step 8 that have been observed. Both of them have been included here. The bani that we are following here is Thanjavur-Pandanallur Bani. There are slight variations in Thanjavur bol and Pandanallur bol. Both of these bol have been accounted here.

The hands are crossed behind the back in pataka hasta. Tattadavu means Tatta (feet or striking of the feet)+ Adavu.

The first Adavu group is based on Tattadavu. The performative sequence is as follows-

- Angikam Shloka
- Prarambhik korvai
- Step 1
- Step 2
- Step 3
- Step 4
- Step 5
- Step 6
- Step 7
- Step 7 Solluketu
- Step 8 Type A
- Step 8 Type B
- Step 8 Solluketu
- Tattadavu Solluketu

Another set performed with Tattadavu is the Chillar Adavu of the basic step of this adavu. The solluketus are not included in this. Only the eight steps are performed. The steps are done once and then the next step follows. Therefore in the original set the right set begins with all the odd numbered steps being performed with the right leg whereas all the even numbered steps are performed with the left leg. The opposite is the case with the left side. All the odd numbered steps are performed with the left leg and all the even numbered steps are performed with the right leg. The chillar adavu is performed in all three speeds. The fourth speed is only performed selectively at the advanced level.

CHAPTER TWO

Angikam Shloka

||Angikam bhuvanam yashya
Vachikam sarva vandgayam
Aharayam chandra taradi
Tvam namah satvikam shivam
Guru brahma guru vishnu
Guru devo maheshvara
Guru sakshat parabrahma
Tatsmay shree guruve namah||

Angikam bhuvanam yashya- The one whose body is this entire world.

Vachikam sarva vandgayam- The one whose voice and words have created the entire literature known.

Aharayam chandra taradi- The one whose jewels are the moon and stars.

Tvam namah satvikam shivam- I fold my hands infront of this magnificent and majestic Shiva.

Guru brahma guru vishnu- (*Guru hi brahma, guru hi vishnu*) The teacher for a student, is no less than God. For a student, his/her guru or teacher is equivalent to Lord Brahma and Lord Vishnu.

Guru devo maheshvara- For a student, his or her guru or teacher is equivalent to all divine forces. His/her guru has been gifted with powers and knowledge that would go beyond the average human being.

Guru sakshat parabrahma- The guru is himself/herself the embodiment of Lord Brahma.

Tatsmay shree guruve namah- I also fold my hands in benevolence in front of my guru, who is equivalent to all divine powers.

Angikam- body (Pataka+Alapadma)

Bhuvanam- world (Suchi+Dolahasta)

Yashya- to be proof/evidence of (Pataka)

Vachikam- voice (Chandrakala)

Sarva vandgayam- entire literature (Pataka)

Aharayam- jewels (Alapadma+Hamsasayog)

Chandra- moon (Ardhachandra)

Taradi- stars (Samdamsho)

Tvam namah- benovelence (Pataka)

Satvikam shivam- magnificent Shiva (Pataka+Shikhara)

Brahma- (Pataka+Mayura)

Vishnu- (Suchi+Dolahasta)

Maheshvara- Natraj pose (Pataka)

Sakshat parabrahma- embodiment of the king of gods, Brahma (Alapadma+Chaturo)

Tatsmay shree guruve namah- benevolence to guru (Anjali)

Mudras used-

- Pataka
- Alapadma
- Suchi
- Dolahasta
- Chandrakala
- Hamsasayog
- Ardhachandra
- Samdamsho
- Shikhara
- Mayura
- Chaturo
- Anjali

Sthanakas used-

- Sthanakam
- Aramandi
- Alida
- Ayatam
- Prenkhadam
- Chalan Chaari
- Ekpadam (Natraj)

CHAPTER THREE

Prarambhik Korvai

||***Kitatak***
Ta Tai Tat Tai
Dhit Tai Tam Tai
Tam Tai Tam||

Prarambhik korvai is performed at the beginning of Adavu groups. It is followed by the steps and preceded by the shloka. This Prarambhik korvai is performed in Aramandi and involves striking the feet following the beats in the given sequence.

---Kitatak------Ta---Tai---Tat---Tai
-Aramandi----(R)---(R)--(L)---(R)
Dhit---Tai---Tam---Tai---Tam---Tai---Tam
(L)*---(R)---(L)----(R)---(L)----(R)---(R)
*Front diagonal prenkhadam

Both Uttarang and Pratyang hands are used for taalam. There are 12 matras in this prarambhik korvai generally.

The 'kitatak' beat is used to take the Aramandi stance and sometimes is counted separately from the performative taalam. Therefore, it can be said that the prarambhik korvai has 11 matras+1 stance beat. The only Uttarang hand used here is the taali used for Kitatak.

Kitatak- Taali
Ta- Sama
Tai- Kanishtha
Tat- Anamika
Tai- Madhyama
Dhit- Sama
Tai- Kanishtha
Tam- Anamika
Tai- Madhyama
Tam- Sama
Tai- Kanishtha
Tam- Anamika

CHAPTER FOUR

STEP 1

|| ***Tai Tai*** ||
or
|| ***Taiya Tai*** ||

Tattadavu 1 includes striking the feet once on each side while sitting in the Aramandi position.

Taiya/Tai---------------------------------Tai
(L)---------------------------------------(R)
Thanjavur Bol- Tai Tai
Pandanallur Bol- Taiya Tai

Vilambha Laya
Taiya/Tai- (L)
Tai- (R)
Taal-Uttarang
Taali- Taiya/Tai
Khaali- Tai

Madhya Laya
Taiya/Tai- (L)
Tai- (R)
Taal-Uttarang
Taali- Taiya/Tai, Tai
Khaali- Taiya/Tai, Tai

Dhurita Laya
Taiya/Tai- (L)
Tai- (R)
Taal-Uttarang
Taali- Taiya/Tai, Tai, Taiya/Tai, Tai
Khaali- Taiya/Tai, Tai, Taiya/Tai, Tai

Anudhurita Laya
Taiya/Tai- (L)
Tai- (R)
Taal-Uttarang
Taali- Taiya/Tai, Tai, Taiya/Tai, Tai, Taiya/Tai, Tai, Taiya/Tai, Tai
Khaali- Taiya/Tai, Tai, Taiya/Tai, Tai, Taiya/Tai, Tai, Taiya/Tai, Tai

CHAPTER FIVE

STEP 2

|| ***Taiya Tai***
Taiya Tai ||

Tattadavu 2 includes striking the feet twice on each side while sitting in the Aramandi position.

Taiya-----Tai--------------------------Taiya-----Tai
(L)-------(L)----------------------------(R)-----(R)

Vilambha Laya

Taiya- (L)
Tai- (L)
Taiya- (R)
Tai- (R)
Taal-Uttarang
Taali- Taiya
Khaali- Tai

Madhya Laya

Taiya- (L)

Tai- (L)
Taiya- (R)
Tai- (R)
Taal-Uttarang
Taali- Taiya, Tai
Khaali- Taiya, Tai

Dhurita Laya

Taiya- (L)
Tai- (L)
Taiya- (R)
Tai- (R)
Taal-Uttarang
Taali- Taiya, Tai, Taiya, Tai
Khaali- Taiya, Tai, Taiya, Tai

Anudhurita Laya

Taiya- (L)
Tai- (L)
Taiya- (R)
Tai- (R)
Taal-Uttarang
Taali- Taiya, Tai, Taiya, Tai, Taiya, Tai, Taiya, Tai
Khaali- Taiya, Tai, Taiya, Tai, Taiya, Tai, Taiya, Tai

CHAPTER SIX

STEP 3

|| ***Taiya Taiya Tam***
Taiya Taiya Tam||

Tattadavu 3 includes striking the feet thrice on each side while sitting in the Aramandi position.

Taiya---Taiya---Tam
(L)-------(L)-----(L)
Taiya---Taiya---Tam
--(R)-----(R)-----(R)
Thanjavur Bol- Tai Tai Tam
Pandanallur Bol- Taiya Taiya Tam

Vilambha Laya

Taiya- (L)
Taiya- (L)
Tam- (L)
Taiya- (R)
Taiya- (R)
Tam- (R)
Taal-Pratyang

Sama- Taiya
Kanishtha- Taiya
Anamika- Tam

Madhya Laya
Taiya- (L)
Taiya- (L)
Tam- (L)
Taiya- (R)
Taiya- (R)
Tam- (R)
Taal-Pratyang
Sama- Taiya, Taiya
Kanishtha- Tam, Taiya
Anamika- Taiya, Tam

Dhurita Laya
Taiya- (L)
Taiya- (L)
Tam- (L)
Taiya- (R)
Taiya- (R)
Tam- (R)
Taal-Pratyang
Sama- Taiya Taiya Tam
Kanishtha- Taiya Taiya Tam
Anamika- Taiya Taiya Tam

Anudhurita Laya
Taiya- (L)

Taiya- (L)
Tam- (L)
Taiya- (R)
Taiya- (R)
Tam (R)
Taal-Pratyang
Sama- Taiya Taiya Tam, Taiya Taiya Tam
Kanishtha- Taiya Taiya Tam, Taiya Taiya Tam
Anamika- Taiya Taiya Tam, Taiya Taiya Tam

CHAPTER SEVEN

STEP 4

|| Taiya Taiya Taiya Tai
Taiya Taiya Taiya Tai||

Tattadavu 4 includes striking the feet four times on each side while sitting in the Aramandi position.

Taiya---Taiya---Taiya---Tai
(L)-------(L)-----(L)-----(L)
Taiya---Taiya---Taiya---Tai
--(R)-----(R)-----(R)----(R)

Vilambha Laya

Taiya- (L)
Taiya- (L)
Taiya- (L)
Tai- (L)
Taiya- (R)
Taiya- (R)
Taiya- (R)
Tai- (R)
Taal-Pratyang

Sama- Taiya
Kanishtha- Taiya
Anamika- Taiya
Madhyama- Tai

Madhya Laya

Taiya- (L)
Taiya- (L)
Taiya- (L)
Tai- (L)
Taiya- (R)
Taiya- (R)
Taiya- (R)
Tai- (R)
Taal-Pratyang
Sama- Taiya Taiya
Kanishtha- Taiya Tai
Anamika- Taiya Taiya
Madhyama- Taiya Tai

Dhurita Laya

Taiya- (L)
Taiya- (L)
Taiya- (L)
Tai- (L)
Taiya- (R)
Taiya- (R)
Taiya- (R)
Tai- (R)
Taal-Pratyang
Sama- Taiya Taiya Taiya Tai

Kanishtha- Taiya Taiya Taiya Tai
Anamika- Taiya Taiya Taiya Tai
Madhyama- Taiya Taiya Taiya Tai

Anudhurita Laya
Taiya- (L)
Taiya- (L)
Taiya- (L)
Tai- (L)
Taiya- (R)
Taiya- (R)
Taiya- (R)
Tai- (R)
Taal-Pratyang
Sama- Taiya Taiya Taiya Tai, Taiya Taiya Taiya Tai
Kanishtha- Taiya Taiya Taiya Tai, Taiya Taiya Taiya Tai
Anamika- Taiya Taiya Taiya Tai, Taiya Taiya Taiya Tai
Madhyama- Taiya Taiya Taiya Tai, Taiya Taiya Taiya Tai

CHAPTER EIGHT

STEP 5

|| ***Taiya Taiya Tai Tai Tam***
Taiya Taiya Tai Tai Tam ||

Tattadavu 5 includes striking the feet five times on each side while sitting in the Aramandi position. The last three beats are done a bit faster. Therefore if the beats were to be numbered as 1, 2, 3, 4, and 5, the performative structure would be 1, 2, (3), (4), (5) where the bracketed beats are done a little faster.

Taiya---Taiya---Tai---Tai---Tam
(L)-------(L)----(L)---(L)---(L)
Taiya---Taiya---Tai---Tai---Tam
(R)-------(R)----(R)---(R)---(R)

Thanjavur Bol- Tai Tai Dhit Dhit Tai or Taiya Taiya Dhit Dhit Tai

Pandanallur Bol- Taiya Taiya Tai Tai Tam

Vilambha Laya

Taiya- (L)
Taiya- (L)

Tai- (L)
Tai- (L)
Tam- (L)
Taiya- (R)
Taiya- (R)
Tai- (R)
Tai- (R)
Tam- (R)
Taal- Uttarang and Pratyang
Taali- Taiya
Khaali- Taiya
Sama- Tai
Kanishtha- Tai
Anamika- Tam

Madhya Laya

Taiya- (L)
Taiya- (L)
Tai- (L)
Tai- (L)
Tam- (L)
Taiya- (R)
Taiya- (R)
Tai- (R)
Tai- (R)
Tam- (R)
Taal- Uttarang and Pratyang
Taali- Taiya Taiya
Khaali- Tai Tai
Sama- Tam Taiya
Kanishtha- Taiya Tai
Anamika- Tai Tam

Dhurita Laya

Taiya- (L)
Taiya (L)
Tai- (L)
Tai- (L)
Tam- (L)
Taiya- (R)
Taiya- (R)
Tai- (R)
Tai- (R)
Tam- (R)
Taal- Uttarang and Pratyang
Taali- Taiya Taiya
Khaali- Tai Tai Tam
Sama- Taiya Taiya
Kanishtha- Tai Tai Tam
Anamika- Taiya Taiya
Taali- Tai Tai Tam
Khaali- Taiya Taiya
Sama- Tai Tai Tam
Kanishtha- Taiya Taiya
Anamika- Tai Tai Tam

Anudhurita Laya

Taiya- (L)
Taiya- (L)
Tai- (L)
Tai- (L)
Tam- (L)
Taiya- (R)

Taiya- (R)
Tai- (R)
Tai- (R)
Tam- (R)
Taal- Uttarang and Pratyang
Taali- Taiya Taiya Tai Tai Tam
Khaali- Taiya Taiya Tai Tai Tam
Sama- Taiya Taiya Tai Tai Tam
Kanishtha- Taiya Taiya Tai Tai Tam
Anamika- Taiya Taiya Tai Tai Tam

CHAPTER NINE

STEP 6

*|| **Taiya Taiya Tam (Kitatak) Taiya Taiya Tam Taiya Taiya Tam (Kitatak) Taiya Taiya Tam** ||*

Tattadavu 6 includes striking the feet six times on each side while sitting in the Aramandi position. There is a pause after the third beat and it is marked with (kitatak).

Taiya---Taiya---Tam--(Kitatak)--Taiya---Taiya---Tam
(L)-------(L)-----(L)-----pause-----(L)------(L)-----(L)
Taiya---Taiya---Tam--(Kitatak)--Taiya---Taiya---Tam
(R)-------(R)-----(R)-----pause-----(R)------(R)-----(R)
Thanjavur Bol- Tai Tai Tam (k) Tai Tai Tam
Pandanallur Bol- Taiya Taiya Tam (k) Taiya Taiya Tam

Vilambha Laya

Taiya- (L)
Taiya- (L)
Tam- (L)
Kitatak- Pause
Taiya- (L)
Taiya- (L)

Tam- (L)
Taiya- (R)
Taiya- (R)
Tam- (R)
Kitatak- Pause
Taiya- (R)
Taiya- (R)
Tam- (R)
Taal-Pratyang
Sama- Taiya
Kanishtha- Taiya
Anamika- Tam (k)
Sama- Taiya
Kanishtha- Taiya
Anamika- Tam (k)

*For the second sama, sama-khaali can be used instead. Usage of both sama and sama-khaali will be correct. Sama-khaali helps to keep the counts on track.

Madhya Laya

Taiya- (L)
Taiya- (L)
Tam- (L)
Kitatak- Pause
Taiya- (L)
Taiya- (L)
Tam- (L)
Taiya- (R)
Taiya- (R)
Tam- (R)
Kitatak- Pause
Taiya- (R)

Taiya- (R)
Tam- (R)
Taal-Pratyang
Sama- Taiya Taya
Kanishtha- Tam (k) Taiya
Anamika- Taiya Tam

*For the second sama, sama-khaali can be used instead. Usage of both sama and sama-khaali will be correct. Sama-khaali helps to keep the counts on track.

Dhurita Laya

Taiya- (L)
Taiya- (L)
Tam- (L)
Kitatak- Pause
Taiya- (L)
Taiya- (L)
Tam- (L)
Taiya- (R)
Taiya- (R)
Tam- (R)
Kitatak- Pause
Taiya- (R)
Taiya- (R)
Tam- (R)
Taal-Pratyang
Sama- Taiya Taiya Tam (k)
Kanishtha- Taiya Taiya Tam
Anamika- Taiya Taiya Tam (k)
Sama- Taiya Taiya Tam
Kanishtha- Taiya Taiya Tam (k)
Anamika- Taiya Taiya Tam

*For the second sama, sama-khaali can be used instead. Usage of both sama and sama-khaali will be correct. Sama-khaali helps to keep the counts on track.

Anudhurita Laya

Taiya- (L)
Taiya- (L)
Tam- (L)
Kitatak- Pause
Taiya- (L)
Taiya- (L)
Tam- (L)
Taiya- (R)
Taiya- (R)
Tam- (R)
Kitatak- Pause
Taiya- (R)
Taiya- (R)
Tam- (R)
Taal-Pratyang
Sama- Taiya Taiya Tam (k) Taiya Taiya Tam
Kanishtha- Taiya Taiya Tam (k) Taiya Taiya Tam
Anamika- Taiya Taiya Tam (k) Taiya Taiya Tam

*For the second sama, sama-khaali can be used instead. Usage of both sama and sama-khaali will be correct. Sama-khaali helps to keep the counts on track.

CHAPTER TEN

STEP 7

|| ***Taiya Taiya Tat Tat Tai Tai Tam***
Taiya Taiya Tat Tat Tai Tai Tam||

Tattadavu 7 includes striking the feet seven times on each side with an exception of the fourth strike being on the opposite side while sitting in the Aramandi position.

Taiya---Taiya---Tat---Tat---Tai---Tai---Tam
(L)-------(L)----(L)---(R)---(L)---(L)---(L)
Taiya---Taiya---Tat---Tat---Tai---Tai---Tam
(R)-------(R)----(R)---(L)---(R)---(R)---(R)
Thanjavur Bol- Tai Tai Tat Tat Tai Tai Tam
Pandanallur Bol- Taiya Taiya Tat Tat Tai Tai Tam

Vilambha Laya

Taiya- (L)
Taiya- (L)
Tat- (L)
Tat- (R)
Tai- (L)
Tai- (L)

Tam- (L)
Taiya- (R)
Taiya- (R)
Tat- (R)
Tat- (L)
Tai- (R)
Tai- (R)
Tam- (R)
Taal-Pratyang
Sama- Taiya
Kanishtha- Taiya
Anamika- Tat
Madhyama- Tat
Sama- Tai
Kanishtha- Tai
Anamika- Tam

*For the second sama, sama-khaali can be used instead. Usage of both sama and sama-khaali will be correct. Sama-khaali helps to keep the counts on track.

Madhya Laya

Taiya- (L)
Taiya- (L)
Tat- (L)
Tat- (R)
Tai- (L)
Tai- (L)
Tam- (L)
Taiya- (R)
Taiya- (R)
Tat- (R)
Tat- (L)

Tai- (R)
Tai- (R)
Tam- (R)
Taal-Pratyang
Sama Taiya Taiya
Kanishtha- Tat Tat
Anamika- Tai Tai
Madhyama- Tam
Sama- Taiya Taiya
Kanishtha- Tat Tat
Anamika- Tai Tai
Sama- Taim
Kanishtha- Taiya Taiya
Anamika- Tat Tat
Madhyama- Tai Tai
Sama- Tam
Kanishtha- Taiya Taiya
Anamika- Tat Tat
Sama- Tai Tai
Kanishtha- Tam
Anamika- Taiya Taiya
Madhyama- Tat Tat
Sama- Tai Tai
Kanishtha- Tam
Anamika- Taiya Taiya
Sama- Tat Tat
Kanishtha- Tai Tai
Anamika- Tam
Madhyama- Taiya Taiya
Sama- Tat Tat
Kanishtha- Tai Tai
Anamika- Tam

*For the second sama, sama-khaali can be used instead. Usage of both sama and sama-khaali will be correct. Sama-khaali helps to keep the counts on track.

Dhurita Laya

Taiya- (L)
Taiya- (L)
Tat- (L)
Tat- (R)
Tai- (L)
Tai- (L)
Tam- (L)
Taiya- (R)
Taiya- (R)
Tat- (R)
Tat- (L)
Tai- (R)
Tai- (R)
Tam- (R)
Taal-Pratyang
Sama- Taiya Taiya Tat Tat
Kanishtha- Tai Tai Tam
Anamika- Taiya Taiya Tat Tat
Madhyama- Tai Tai Tam
Sama- Taiya Taiya Tat Tat
Kanishtha- Tai Tai Tam
Anamika- Taiya Taiya Tat Tat
Sama- Tai Tai Tam
Kanishtha- Taiya Taiya Tat Tat
Anamika- Tai Tai Tam
Madhyama- Taiya Taiya Tat Tat
Sama- Tai Tai Tam

Kanishtha- Taiya Taiya Tat Tat
Anamika- Tai Tai Tam

*For the second sama, sama-khaali can be used instead. Usage of both sama and sama-khaali will be correct. Sama-khaali helps to keep the counts on track.

Anudhurita Laya

Taiya- (L)
Taiya- (L)
Tat- (L)
Tat- (R)
Tai- (L)
Tai- (L)
Tam- (L)
Taiya- (R)
Taiya- (R)
Tat- (R)
Tat- (L)
Tai- (R)
Tai- (R)
Tam- (R)
Taal-Pratyang
Sama- Taiya Taiya Tat Tat Tai Tai Tam
Kanishtha- Taiya Taiya Tat Tat Tai Tai Tam
Anamika- Taiya Taiya Tat Tat Tai Tai Tam
Madhyama- Taiya Taiya Tat Tat Tai Tai Tam
Sama- Taiya Taiya Tat Tat Tai Tai Tam
Kanishtha- Taiya Taiya Tat Tat Tai Tai Tam
Anamika- Taiya Taiya Tat Tat Tai Tai Tam

*For the second sama, sama-khaali can be used instead. Usage of both sama and sama-khaali will be correct. Sama-khaali helps to keep the counts on track.

CHAPTER ELEVEN

STEP 7 SOLLUKETU

|| ***Tai Tai Tai Tai Tai Tai Tam Tai Tai Tam***
Tai Tai Tai Tai Tai Tai Tam Tai Tai Tam**||**

Tattadavu 7 Solluketu includes striking the feet four times on each side while sitting in the Aramandi position. It is followed by back 'dhit dhit tai' while using Swastikam and Aramandi.

Tai---Tai---Tai---Tai---Tai---Tai---Tam---Tai---Tai---Tam
(L)---(L)--(L)---(L)---(R)---(L)---(R)---(L)---(R)---(L)
----------------------------dhit-dhit-tai-------dhit-dhit-tai---
Tai---Tai---Tai---Tai---Tai---Tai---Tam---Tai---Tai---Tam
(R)---(R)--(R)---(R)---(L)---(R)---(L)---(R)---(L)---(R)
----------------------------dhit-dhit-tai-------dhit-dhit-tai---

Thanjavur Bol- Tai Tai Tai Tai Tai Tai Tam Tai Tai Tam

Pandanallur Bol- Taiya Tai Taiya Tai Tai Tai Tam Tai Tai Tam

Vilambha Laya

Tai- (L)
Tai- (L)

Tai- (L)
Tai- (L)
Tai- (R)
Tai- (L)
Tam (R)
Tai- (L)
Tai- (R)
Tam- (L)
Tai- (R)
Tai- (R)
Tai- (R)
Tai- (R)
Tai- (L)
Tai- (R)
Tam- (L)
Tai- (R)
Tai- (L)
Tam- (R)
Taal-Uttarang and Pratyang
Taali- Tai
Khaali- Tai
Taali- Tai
Khaali- Tai
Sama- Tai
Kanishtha- Tai
Anamika- Tam
Sama- Tai
Kanishtha- Tai
Anamika- Tam

*For the second sama, sama-khaali can be used instead. Usage of both sama and sama-khaali will be correct. Sama-khaali helps to keep the counts on track.

Madhya Laya

Tai- (L)
Tai- (L)
Tai- (L)
Tai- (L)
Tai- (R)
Tai- (L)
Tam- (R)
Tai- (L)
Tai- (R)
Tam- (L)
Tai- (R)
Tai- (R)
Tai- (R)
Tai- (R)
Tai- (L)
Tai- (R)
Tam- (L)
Tai- (R)
Tai- (L)
Tam- (R)

Taal-Uttarang and Pratyang

Taali- Tai Tai
Khaali- Tai Tai
Taali- Tai Tai
Khaali- Tam Tai
Sama- Tai Tam
Kanishtha- Tai Tai
Anamika- Tai Tai
Sama- Tai Tai
Kanishtha- Tam Tai
Anamika- Tai Tam

*For the second sama, sama-khaali can be used instead. Usage of both sama and sama-khaali will be correct. Sama-khaali helps to keep the counts on track.

Dhurita Laya

Tai- (L)
Tai- (L)
Tai- (L)
Tai- (L)
Tai- (R)
Tai- (L)
Tam- (R)
Tai- (L)
Tai- (R)
Tam- (L)
Tai- (R)
Tai- (R)
Tai- (R)
Tai- (R)
Tai- (L)
Tai- (R)
Tam- (L)
Tai- (R)
Tai- (L)
Tam- (R)
Taal-Uttarang and Pratyang
Taali- Tai Tai
Khaali- Tai Tai
Taali- Tai Tai Tam
Khaali- Tai Tai Tam
Sama- Tai Tai
Kanishtha- Tai Tai

Anamika- Tai Tai Tam
Sama- Tai Tai Tam
Kanishtha- Tai Tai
Anamika- Tai Tai
Taali- Tai Tai Tam
Khaali- Tai Tai Tam
Taali- Tai Tai
Khaali- Tai Tai
Sama- Tai Tai Tam
Kanishtha- Tai Tai Tam
Anamika- Tai Tai
Sama- Tai Tai
Kanishtha- Tai Tai Tam
Anamika- Tai Tai Tam

*For the second sama, sama-khaali can be used instead. Usage of both sama and sama-khaali will be correct. Sama-khaali helps to keep the counts on track.

Anudhurita Laya

Tai- (L)
Tai- (L)
Tai- (L)
Tai- (L)
Tai- (R)
Tai- (L)
Tam- (R)
Tai- (L)
Tai- (R)
Tam- (L)
Tai- (R)
Tai- (R)
Tai- (R)

Tai- (R)
Tai- (L)
Tai- (R)
Tam- (L)
Tai- (R)
Tai- (L)
Tam- (R)
Taal-Uttarang and Pratyang
Taali- Tai Tai Tai Tai
Khaali- Tai Tai Tam Tai Tai Tam
Taali- Tai Tai Tai Tai
Khaali- Tai Tai Tam Tai Tai Tam
Sama- Tai Tai Tai Tai
Kanishtha- Tai Tai Tam Tai Tai Tam
Anamika- Tai Tai Tai Tai
Sama- Tai Tai Tam Tai Tai Tam
Kanishtha- Tai Tai Tai Tai
Anamika- Tai Tai Tam Tai Tai Tam

*For the second sama, sama-khaali can be used instead. Usage of both sama and sama-khaali will be correct. Sama-khaali helps to keep the counts on track.

CHAPTER TWELVE

STEP 8A

|| ***Taiya Taiya Taiya Tai Dhit Dhit Tai***
Taiya Taiya Taiya Tai Dhit Dhit Tai ||

Tattadavu 8 has two variants. The first variant includes striking the feet seven times on alternate sides while sitting in the Aramandi position. The 'dhit dhit tai' segment is a bit faster than the initial four beats. Counting the beats, we find that there are only seven there. the eighth beat is supposed to be blank.

Taiya--Taiya--Taiya--Tai---Dhit--Dhit--Tai
(L)------(R)----(L)----(R)---(L)---(R)---(L)
Taiya--Taiya--Taiya--Tai---Dhit--Dhit--Tai
(R)------(L)----(R)----(L)---(R)---(L)---(R)
Thanjavur Bol- Tai Tai Tai Tai Dhit Dhit Tai
Pandanallur Bol- Taiya Taiya Taiya Tai Dhit Dhit Tai

Vilambha Laya

Taiya- (L)
Taiya- (R)
Taiya- (L)

Tai- (R)
Dhit- (L)
Dhit- (R)
Tai- (L)
Taiya- (R)
Taiya- (L)
Taiya- (R)
Tai- (L)
Dhit- (R)
Dhit- (L)
Tai- (R)
Taal-Pratyang
Sama- Taiya
Kanishtha- Taiya
Anamika- Taiya
Madhyama- Tai
Sama- Dhit
Kanishtha- Dhit
Anamika- Tai

*For the second sama, sama-khaali can be used instead. Usage of both sama and sama-khaali will be correct. Sama-khaali helps to keep the counts on track.

Madhya Laya

Taiya- (L)
Taiya- (R)
Taiya- (L)
Tai- (R)
Dhit- (L)
Dhit- (R)
Tai- (L)
Taiya- (R)

Taiya- (L)
Taiya- (R)
Tai- (L)
Dhit- (R)
Dhit- (L)
Tai- (R)
Taal-Pratyang
Sama- Taiya Taiya
Kanishtha- Taiya Tai
Anamika- Dhit Dhit
Madhyama- Tai
Sama- Taiya Taiya
Kanishtha- Taiya Tai
Anamika- Dhit Dhit
Sama- Tai
Kanishtha- Taiya Taiya
Anamika- Taiya Tai
Madhyama- Dhit Dhit
Sama- Tai
Kanishtha- Taiya Taiya
Anamika- Taiya Tai
Sama- Dhit Dhit
Kanishtha- Tai
Anamika- Taiya Taiya
Madhyama- Taiya Tai
Sama-Dhit Dhit
Kanishtha- Tai
Anamika- Taiya Taiya
Sama- Taiya Tai
Kanishtha- Dhit Dhit
Anamika- Tai
Madhyama- Taiya Taiya
Sama- Taiya Tai

Kanishtha- Dhit Dhit

Anamika- Tai

*For the second sama, sama-khaali can be used instead. Usage of both sama and sama-khaali will be correct. Sama-khaali helps to keep the counts on track.

Dhurita Laya

Taiya- (L)
Taiya- (R)
Taiya- (L)
Tai- (R)
Dhit- (L)
Dhit- (R)
Tai- (L)
Taiya- (R)
Taiya- (L)
Taiya- (R)
Tai- (L)
Dhit- (R)
Dhit- (L)
Tai- (R)

Taal-Pratyang

Sama- Taiya Taiya
Kanishtha- Taiya Tai
Anamika- Dhit Dhit Tai
Madhyama- Taiya Taiya
Sama- Taiya Tai
Kanishtha- Dhit Dhit Tai
Anamika- Taiya Taiya
Sama- Taiya Tai
Kanishtha- Dhit Dhit Tai
Anamika- Taiya Taiya

Madhyama- Taiya Tai
Sama- Dhit Dhit Tai
Kanishtha-Taiya Taiya
Anamika- Taiya Tai
Sama- Dhit Dhit Tai
Kanishtha- Taiya Taiya
Anamika- Taiya Tai
Madhyama- Dhit Dhit Tai
Sama- Taiya Taiya
Kanishtha- Taiya Tai
Anamika- Dhit Dhit Tai

*For the second sama, sama-khaali can be used instead. Usage of both sama and sama-khaali will be correct. Sama-khaali helps to keep the counts on track.

Anudhurita Laya

Taiya- (L)
Taiya- (R)
Taiya- (L)
Tai- (R)
Dhit- (L)
Dhit- (R)
Tai- (L)
Taiya- (R)
Taiya- (L)
Taiya- (R)
Tai- (L)
Dhit- (R)
Dhit- (L)
Tai- (R)
Taal-Pratyang
Sama- Taiya Taiya Taiya Tai

Kanishtha- Dhit Dhit Tai
Anamika- Taiya Taiya Taiya Tai
Madhyama- Dhit Dhit Tai
Sama- Taiya Taiya Taiya Tai
Kanishtha- Dhit Dhit Tai
Anamika- Taiya Taiya Taiya Tai
Sama- Dhit Dhit Tai
Kanishtha- Taiya Taiya Taiya Tai
Anamika- Dhit Dhit Tai
Madhyama- Taiya Taiya Taiya Tai
Sama- Dhit Dhit Tai
Kanishtha- Taiya Taiya Taiya Tai
Anamika- Dhit Dhit Tai

*For the second sama, sama-khaali can be used instead. Usage of both sama and sama-khaali will be correct. Sama-khaali helps to keep the counts on track.

CHAPTER THIRTEEN

STEP 8B

|| *Taiya Taiya Tam Taiya Taiya Dhit Dhit Tai*
***Taiya Taiya Tam Taiya Taiya Dhit Dhit Tai*||**

Tattadavu 8 has two variants. The second variant includes striking the feet seven times in a given combination while sitting in the Aramandi position. The 'dhit dhit tai' segment is a bit faster than the initial four beats. This variant is preferred over the first one because it has eight countable beats as taalam.

Taiya--Taiya--Tam--Taiya--Taiya--Dhit--Dhit--Tai
(L)------(L)----(R)----(L)----(R)----(L)---(R)---(L)
Taiya--Taiya--Tam--Taiya--Taiya--Dhit--Dhit--Tai
(R)------(R)----(L)----(R)----(L)----(R)---(L)---(R)
Thanjavur Bol- Tai Tai Tam Tai Tai Dhit Dhit Tai
Pandanallur Bol- Taiya Taiya Tam Taiya Taiya Dhit Dhit Tai

Vilambha Laya

Taiya- (L)
Taiya- (L)

Tam- (R)
Taiya- (L)
Taiya- (R)
Dhit- (L)
Dhit- (R)
Tai- (L)
Taiya- (R)
Taiya- (R)
Tam- (L)
Taiya- (R)
Tai- (L)
Dhit- (R)
Dhit- (L)
Tai- (R)
Taal-Uttarang andPratyang
Sama- Taiya
Kanishtha- Taiya
Anamika- Tam
Taali- Taiya
Khaali- Taiya
Sama- Dhit
Kanishtha- Dhit
Anamika- Tai

*For the second sama, sama-khaali can be used instead. Usage of both sama and sama-khaali will be correct. Sama-khaali helps to keep the counts on track.

Madhya Laya
Taiya- (L)
Taiya- (L)
Tam- (R)
Taiya- (L)

Taiya- (R)
Dhit- (L)
Dhit- (R)
Tai- (L)
Taiya- (R)
Taiya- (R)
Tam- (L)
Taiya- (R)
Tai- (L)
Dhit- (R)
Dhit- (L)
Tai- (R)
Taal-Uttarang andPratyang
Sama- Taiya Taiya
Kanishtha- Tam
Anamika- Taiya Taiya
Taali- Dhit Dhit Tai
Khaali- Taiya Taiya
Sama- Tam
Kanishtha- Taiya Taiya
Anamika- Dhit Dhit Tai

*For the second sama, sama-khaali can be used instead. Usage of both sama and sama-khaali will be correct. Sama-khaali helps to keep the counts on track.

Dhurita Laya
Taiya- (L)
Taiya- (L)
Tam- (R)
Taiya- (L)
Taiya- (R)
Dhit- (L)

Dhit- (R)
Tai- (L)
Taiya- (R)
Taiya- (R)
Tam- (L)
Taiya- (R)
Tai- (L)
Dhit- (R)
Dhit- (L)
Tai- (R)
Taal-Uttarang andPratyang
Sama- Taiya Taiya Tam
Kanishtha- Taiya Taiya Dhit Dhit Tai
Anamika- Taiya Taiya Tam
Taali- Taiya Taiya Dhit Dhit Tai
Khaali- Taiya Taiya Tam
Sama- Taiya Taiya Dhit Dhit Tai
Kanishtha- Taiya Taiya Tam
Anamika- Taiya Taiya Dhit Dhit Tai

*For the second sama, sama-khaali can be used instead. Usage of both sama and sama-khaali will be correct. Sama-khaali helps to keep the counts on track.

Anudhurita Laya

Taiya- (L)
Taiya- (L)
Tam- (R)
Taiya- (L)
Taiya- (R)
Dhit- (L)
Dhit- (R)
Tai- (L)

Taiya- (R)
Taiya- (R)
Tam- (L)
Taiya- (R)
Tai- (L)
Dhit- (R)
Dhit- (L)
Tai- (R)
Taal-Uttarang andPratyang
Sama- Taiya Taiya Tam Taiya Taiya Dhit Dhit Tai
Kanishtha- Taiya Taiya Tam Taiya Taiya Dhit Dhit Tai
Anamika- Taiya Taiya Tam Taiya Taiya Dhit Dhit Tai
Taali- Taiya Taiya Tam Taiya Taiya Dhit Dhit Tai
Khaali- Taiya Taiya Tam Taiya Taiya Dhit Dhit Tai
Sama- Taiya Taiya Tam Taiya Taiya Dhit Dhit Tai
Kanishtha- Taiya Taiya Tam Taiya Taiya Dhit Dhit Tai
Anamika- Taiya Taiya Tam Taiya Taiya Dhit Dhit Tai

*For the second sama, sama-khaali can be used instead. Usage of both sama and sama-khaali will be correct. Sama-khaali helps to keep the counts on track.

CHAPTER FOURTEEN

STEP 8 SOLLUKETU

|| ***Tai Tai Tai Tai Tai Tai Tam Tai Tai Tam***
Tai Tai Tai Tai Tai Tai Tam Tai Tai Tam||

Tattadavu 8 Solluketu includes striking the feet four times on each side while sitting in the Aramandi position. It is followed by front 'dhit dhit tai' while using Prenkhadam and Aramandi.

Tai---Tai---Tai---Tai---Tai---Tai---Tam---Tai---Tai---Tam
(L)---(L)--(L)---(L)---(R)---(L)---(R)---(L)---(R)---(L)
----------------------------dhit-dhit-tai-------dhit-dhit-tai---
Tai---Tai---Tai---Tai---Tai---Tai---Tam---Tai---Tai---Tam
(R)---(R)--(R)---(R)---(L)---(R)---(L)---(R)---(L)---(R)
----------------------------dhit-dhit-tai-------dhit-dhit-tai---

Thanjavur Bol- Tai Tai Tai Tai Tai Tai Tam Tai Tai Tam

Pandanallur Bol- Taiya Tai Taiya Tai Tai Tai Tam Tai Tai Tam

Vilambha Laya
Tai- (L)
Tai- (L)
Tai- (L)
Tai- (L)
Tai- (R)
Tai- (L)
Tam- (R)
Tai- (L)
Tai- (R)
Tam- (L)
Tai- (R)
Tai- (R)
Tai- (R)
Tai- (R)
Tai- (L)
Tai- (R)
Tam- (L)
Tai- (R)
Tai- (L)
Tam- (R)
Taal-Uttarang and Pratyang
Taali- Tai
Khaali- Tai
Taali- Tai
Khaali- Tai
Sama- Tai
Kanishtha- Tai
Anamika- Tam
Sama- Tai
Kanishtha- Tai
Anamika- Tam

*For the second sama, sama-khaali can be used instead. Usage of both sama and sama-khaali will be correct. Sama-khaali helps to keep the counts on track.

Madhya Laya
Tai- (L)
Tai- (L)
Tai- (L)
Tai- (L)
Tai- (R)
Tai- (L)
Tam- (R)
Tai- (L)
Tai- (R)
Tam- (L)
Tai- (R)
Tai- (R)
Tai- (R)
Tai- (R)
Tai- (L)
Tai- (R)
Tam- (L)
Tai- (R)
Tai- (L)
Tam- (R)
Taal-Uttarang and Pratyang
Taali- Tai Tai
Khaali- Tai Tai
Taali- Tai Tai
Khaali- Tam Tai

Sama- Tai Tam
Kanishtha- Tai Tai
Anamika- Tai Tai
Sama- Tai Tai
Kanishtha- Tam Tai
Anamika- Tai Tam

*For the second sama, sama-khaali can be used instead. Usage of both sama and sama-khaali will be correct. Sama-khaali helps to keep the counts on track.

Dhurita Laya
Tai- (L)
Tai- (L)
Tai- (L)
Tai- (L)
Tai- (R)
Tai- (L)
Tam- (R)
Tai- (L)
Tai- (R)
Tam- (L)
Tai- (R)
Tai- (R)
Tai- (R)
Tai- (R)
Tai- (L)
Tai- (R)
Tam- (L)
Tai- (R)
Tai- (L)

Tam- (R)
Taal-Uttarang and Pratyang
Taali- Tai Tai
Khaali- Tai Tai
Taali- Tai Tai Tam
Khaali- Tai Tai Tam
Sama- Tai Tai
Kanishtha- Tai Tai
Anamika- Tai Tai Tam
Sama- Tai Tai Tam
Kanishtha- Tai Tai
Anamika- Tai Tai
Taali- Tai Tai Tam
Khaali- Tai Tai Tam
Taali- Tai Tai
Khaali- Tai Tai
Sama- Tai Tai Tam
Kanishtha- Tai Tai Tam
Anamika- Tai Tai
Sama- Tai Tai
Kanishtha- Tai Tai Tam
Anamika- Tai Tai Tam

*For the second sama, sama-khaali can be used instead. Usage of both sama and sama-khaali will be correct. Sama-khaali helps to keep the counts on track.

Anudhurita Laya
Tai- (L)
Tai- (L)
Tai- (L)

Tai- (L)
Tai- (R)
Tai- (L)
Tam- (R)
Tai- (L)
Tai- (R)
Tam- (L)
Tai- (R)
Tai- (R)
Tai- (R)
Tai- (R)
Tai- (L)
Tai- (R)
Tam- (L)
Tai- (R)
Tai- (L)
Tam- (R)
Taal-Uttarang and Pratyang
Taali- Tai Tai Tai Tai
Khaali- Tai Tai Tam Tai Tai Tam
Taali- Tai Tai Tai Tai
Khaali- Tai Tai Tam Tai Tai Tam
Sama- Tai Tai Tai Tai
Kanishtha- Tai Tai Tam Tai Tai Tam
Anamika- Tai Tai Tai Tai
Sama- Tai Tai Tam Tai Tai Tam
Kanishtha- Tai Tai Tai Tai
Anamika- Tai Tai Tam Tai Tai Tam

*For the second sama, sama-khaali can be used instead. Usage of both sama and sama-khaali will be correct. Sama-khaali helps to keep the counts on track.

CHAPTER FIFTEEN

Tattadavu Solluketu

|| Taiya Taiya Tam Taiya Taiya Tam
Tai Tai Tat Ta Dhit Tai Tat Ta
Taiya Taiya Tam Taiya Taiya Tam
Tai Tai Tat Ta Dhit Tai Tat Ta
Tam Tai Tai Tam Tam Tai Tai Tam
Tai Tai Tat Ta Dhit Tai Tat Ta
Tam Tai Tai Tam Tam Tai Tai Tam
Tai Tai Tat Ta Dhit Tai Tat Ta
Tam Tam Tai Tam Tam Tam Tai Tam
Tai Tai Tat Ta Dhit Tai Tat Ta
Tam Tam Tai Tam Tam Tam Tai Tam
Tai Tai Tat Ta Dhit Tai Tat Ta
Tam Tam Tam Tam Tam Tam
Tai Tai Tat Ta Dhit Tai Tat Ta
Tam Tam Tam Tam Tam Tam
Tai Tai Tat Ta Dhit Tai Tat Ta||

This is the solluketu of Adavu Group 1 (Tattadavu) and is performed by the end of the group. It can be classified into four segments. The portion "Tai tai tat ta, dhit tai tat ta" is repeated often. For this step, the dancer slides his/her feet in one direction making a semi-circular movement. This is to be done for the matra "Ta" (and 'dhit respectively). The dancer strikes the feet at the matra "Tai". For "Tat-Ta", standing-swastikam is made and both feet are struck respectively. Hands are kept crossed behind the back in Pataka hasta throughout this.

Taiya--Taiya--Tam---Taiya--Taiya--Tam
(R)-----(R)----(R)-----(L)----(L)-----(L)
Tai-----Tai---Tat---Ta----Dhit---Tai--- Tat---Ta
slide---(R)---(L)--(R)---slide---(L)---(R)---(L)
Taiya--Taiya--Tam---Taiya--Taiya--Tam
(R)-----(R)----(R)-----(L)----(L)-----(L)
Tai-----Tai---Tat---Ta----Dhit---Tai--- Tat---Ta
slide---(R)---(L)--(R)---slide---(L)---(R)---(L)
Tam---Tai---Tai---Tam---Tam---Tai---Tai---Tam
-(R)---(L)---(L)---(R)-----(L)---(R)---(R)---(L)
Tai-----Tai---Tat---Ta----Dhit---Tai--- Tat---Ta
slide---(R)---(L)--(R)---slide---(L)---(R)---(L)
Tam---Tai---Tai---Tam---Tam---Tai---Tai---Tam
-(R)---(L)---(L)---(R)-----(L)---(R)---(R)---(L)
Tai-----Tai---Tat---Ta----Dhit---Tai--- Tat---Ta
slide---(R)---(L)--(R)---slide---(L)---(R)---(L)
Tam---Tam---Tai---Tam---Tam---Tam---Tai---Tam
-(R)----(R)---(L)----(R)----(L)-----(L)---(R)---(L)
Tai-----Tai---Tat---Ta----Dhit---Tai--- Tat---Ta
slide---(R)---(L)--(R)---slide---(L)---(R)---(L)
Tam---Tam---Tai---Tam---Tam---Tam---Tai---Tam
-(R)----(R)---(L)----(R)----(L)-----(L)---(R)---(L)
Tai-----Tai---Tat---Ta----Dhit---Tai--- Tat---Ta

slide---(R)---(L)--(R)---slide---(L)---(R)---(L)
Tam---Tam---Tam---Tam---Tam---Tam
-(R)----(L)----(R)----(L)-----(R)----(L)
Tai-----Tai---Tat---Ta----Dhit---Tai--- Tat---Ta
slide---(R)---(L)--(R)---slide---(L)---(R)---(L)
Tam---Tam---Tam---Tam---Tam---Tam
-(R)----(L)----(R)----(L)-----(R)----(L)
Tai-----Tai---Tat---Ta----Dhit---Tai--- Tat---Ta
slide---(R)---(L)--(R)---slide---(L)---(R)---(L)

Hands for the common portion "Tai Tai Tat Ta, Dhit Tai Tat Ta" the hands are as follows-

Pratyang
Tai- Sama
Tai- Kanishtha
Tat-Anamika
Ta- Madhyama
Dhit- Sama
Tai- Kanishtha
Tat- Anamika
Ta- Madhyama

Hands for Segment 1- "Taiya Taiya Tam" are as follows-

Pratyang
Taiya- Sama
Taiya- Kanishtha
Tam- Anamika

Hands for Segment 2- "Tam Tai Tai Tam" are as follows-

Pratyang

Tam- Sama

Tai- Kanishtha

Tai- Anamika

Tam- Madhyama

Hands for Segment 3- "Tam Tam Tai Tam" are as follows-

Pratyang

Tam- Sama

Tam- Kanishtha

Tai- Anamika

Tam- Madhyama

Hands for Segment 4- "Tam Tam Tam" are as follows-

Pratyang

Tam- Sama

Tam- Knishtha

Tam- Anamika

CHAPTER SIXTEEN

ADAVU GROUP 1

Angikam

Angikam bhuvanam yashya
Vachikam sarva vandgayam
Aharayam chandra taradi
Tvam namah satvikam shivam
Guru brahma guru vishnu
Guru devo maheshvara
Guru sakshat parabrahma
Tatsmay shree guruve namah

Prarambhik Korvai

Kitatak
Ta Tai Tat Tai
Dhit Tai Tam Tai
Tam Tai Tam

Step 1

Kitatak
Tai Tai (Vilambha laya)
Tai Tai (Madhya laya)
Tai Tai (Dhurita laya)

Step 2

Taiya Tai, Taiya Tai (Vilambha laya)
Taiya Tai, Taiya Tai (Madhya laya)

Taiya Tai, Taiya Tai (Dhurita laya)

Step 3

Taiya Taiya Tam, Taiya Taiya Tam (Vilambha laya)

Taiya Taiya Tam, Taiya Taiya Tam (Madhya laya)

Taiya Taiya Tam, Taiya Taiya Tam (Dhurita laya)

Step 4

Taiya Taiya Taiya Tai, Taiya Taiya Taiya Tai (Vilambha laya)

Taiya Taiya Taiya Tai, Taiya Taiya Taiya Tai (Madhya laya)

Taiya Taiya Taiya Tai, Taiya Taiya Taiya Tai (Dhurita laya)

Step 5

Taiya Taiya Tai Tai Tam, Taiya Taiya Tai Tai Tam (Vilambha laya)

Taiya Taiya Tai Tai Tam, Taiya Taiya Tai Tai Tam (Madhya laya)

Taiya Taiya Tai Tai Tam, Taiya Taiya Tai Tai Tam (Dhurita laya)

Step 6

Taiya Taiya Tam (Kitatak) Taiya Taiya Tam, Taiya Taiya Tam (Kitatak) Taiya Taiya Tam (Vilambha laya)

Taiya Taiya Tam (Kitatak) Taiya Taiya Tam, Taiya Taiya Tam (Kitatak) Taiya Taiya Tam (Madhya laya)

Taiya Taiya Tam (Kitatak) Taiya Taiya Tam, Taiya Taiya Tam (Kitatak) Taiya Taiya Tam (Dhurita laya)

Step 7

Taiya Taiya Tat Tat Tai Tai Tam, Taiya Taiya Tat Tat Tai Tai Tam (Vilambha laya)

Taiya Taiya Tat Tat Tai Tai Tam, Taiya Taiya Tat Tat Tai Tai Tam (Madhya laya)

Taiya Taiya Tat Tat Tai Tai Tam, Taiya Taiya Tat Tat Tai Tai Tam (Dhurita laya)

Step 7 Solluketu

Tai Tai Tai Tai Tai Tai Tam Tai Tai Tam, Tai Tai Tai Tai Tai Tai Tam Tai Tai Tam (Vilambha laya)

Tai Tai Tai Tai Tai Tai Tam Tai Tai Tam, Tai Tai Tai Tai Tai Tai Tam Tai Tai Tam (Madhya laya)

Tai Tai Tai Tai Tai Tai Tam Tai Tai Tam, Tai Tai Tai Tai Tai Tai Tam Tai Tai Tam (Dhurita laya)

Step 8A

Taiya Taiya Taiya Tai Dhit Dhit Tai, Taiya Taiya Taiya Tai Dhit Dhit Tai (Vilambha laya)

Taiya Taiya Taiya Tai Dhit Dhit Tai, Taiya Taiya Taiya Tai Dhit Dhit Tai (Madhya laya)

Taiya Taiya Taiya Tai Dhit Dhit Tai, Taiya Taiya Taiya Tai Dhit Dhit Tai (Dhurita laya)

Step 8B

Taiya Taiya Tam Taiya Taiya Dhit Dhit Tai, Taiya Taiya Tam Taiya Taiya Dhit Dhit Tai (Vilambha laya)

Taiya Taiya Tam Taiya Taiya Dhit Dhit Tai, Taiya Taiya Tam Taiya Taiya Dhit Dhit Tai (Madhya laya)

Taiya Taiya Tam Taiya Taiya Dhit Dhit Tai, Taiya Taiya Tam Taiya Taiya Dhit Dhit Tai (Dhurita laya)

Step 8 Solluketu

Tai Tai Tai Tai Tai Tai Tam Tai Tai Tam, Tai Tai Tai Tai Tai Tai Tam Tai Tai Tam (Vilambha laya)

Tai Tai Tai Tai Tai Tai Tam Tai Tai Tam, Tai Tai Tai Tai Tai Tai Tam Tai Tai Tam (Madhya laya)

Tai Tai Tai Tai Tai Tai Tam Tai Tai Tam, Tai Tai Tai Tai Tai Tai Tam Tai Tai Tam (Dhurita laya)

Tattadavu Solluketu

Taiya Taiya Tam Taiya Taiya Tam

Tai Tai Tat Ta Dhit Tai Tat Ta

Taiya Taiya Tam Taiya Taiya Tam

Tai Tai Tat Ta Dhit Tai Tat Ta

Tam Tai Tai Tam Tam Tai Tai Tam
Tai Tai Tat Ta Dhit Tai Tat Ta
Tam Tai Tai Tam Tam Tai Tai Tam
Tai Tai Tat Ta Dhit Tai Tat Ta
Tam Tam Tai Tam Tam Tam Tai Tam
Tai Tai Tat Ta Dhit Tai Tat Ta
Tam Tam Tai Tam Tam Tam Tai Tam
Tai Tai Tat Ta Dhit Tai Tat Ta
Tam Tam Tam Tam Tam Tam
Tai Tai Tat Ta Dhit Tai Tat Ta
Tam Tam Tam Tam Tam Tam
Tai Tai Tat Ta Dhit Tai Tat Ta

CHAPTER SEVENTEEN

CHILLAR TATTADAVU

Taiya
Taiya Tai
Taiya Taiya Tam
Taiya Taiya Taiya Tai
Taiya Taiya Tai Tai Tam
Taiya Taiya Tam (kitatak) Taiya Taiya Tam
Taiya Taiya Tat Tat Tai Tai Tam
Taiya Taiya Tam Taiya Taiya Dhit Dhit Tai

Right Side

R-Taiya
L-Taiya Tai
R-Taiya Taiya Tam
L-Taiya Taiya Taiya Tai
R-Taiya Taiya Tai Tai Tam
L-Taiya Taiya Tam (kitatak) Taiya Taiya Tam
R-Taiya Taiya Tat Tat Tai Tai Tam
L-Taiya Taiya Tam Taiya Taiya Dhit Dhit Tai

Left Side
L-Taiya
R-Taiya Tai
L-Taiya Taiya Tam
R-Taiya Taiya Taiya Tai
L-Taiya Taiya Tai Tai Tam
R-Taiya Taiya Tam (kitatak) Taiya Taiya Tam
L-Taiya Taiya Tat Tat Tai Tai Tam
R-Taiya Taiya Tam Taiya Taiya Dhit Dhit Tai

Hands
Taiya- Taali

.

Taiya- Taali
Tai- Khaali

.

Taiya- Sama
Taiya- Kanishtha
Tam-Anamika

.

Taiya- Sama
Taiya- Kanishtha
Taiya- Anamika
Tai- Madhyama

.

Taiya- Taali
Taiya- Khaali
Tai- Sama
Tai- Kanishtha
Tam- Anamika

.

Taiya- Sama
Taiya- Kanishtha
Tam- Anamika
(kitatak)
Taiya- Sama (Sama-khaali)
Taiya- Kanishtha
Tam- Anamika
.
Taiya- Sama
Taiya- Kanishtha
Tat- Anamika
Tat- Madhyama
Tai- Sama (Sama-khaali)
Tai- Kanishtha
Tam- Anamika
.
Taiya- Sama
Taiya- Kanishtha
Tam- Anamika
Taiya- Taali
Taiya- Khaali
Dhit- Sama (Sama-khaali)
Dhit- Kanishtha
Tai- Anamika

Nrityangana Kala Kendra Bharatnatyam Level 1 Part A

The forms for Bharatnatyam Level 1 Part A are available online. You can visit the store- *edu.nrityanganakalakendra.com* to purchase and submit the form.

The syllabus includes-

Module 1: Theoretical Foundation

Module 2: Bhedas

Module 3: Shlokas

Module 4: Adavus I

Module 5: Adavus II

Module 6: Pushpanjali

(This book is a part of the curriculum of Module 4)

For any queries send an email at *nrityanganakalakendra.edu@gmail.com*.

9 798887 492681

Printed by Libri Plureos GmbH in Hamburg,
Germany